"Tim Chester and Katy Morgan want teenagers to know that Christianity is all about *Jesus*. They faithfully contextualize the gospel into language relatable to teenagers by defining biblical terms, asking meaningful questions, and providing plenty of teaching tools for group leaders. Meanwhile, they resist the urge to sacrifice on substance. The result is a study that will be accessible for all the students in your youth group—from skeptics and new believers to committed Christians—as they grow in knowing Christ."

CHELSEA KINGSTON ERICKSON, Director of Publishing,
Rooted Ministry; former youth worker

"What does life with Jesus actually look like? It's easy to say, 'I'm a Christian', but what does that mean for your life, your suffering, your relationships, your faith in God? *Life with Jesus: Youth Edition* is a fantastic resource for any young person serious about growing in their faith. You'll love how this book helps you live life to the full as a disciple of Jesus. Gather a group, open the Bible, ask questions, hear real-life stories, and prepare to let God work in and change you. Go on, give it a go!"

DAVE CORNES, Associate Youth Evangelist,
Christianity Explored Ministries

"If you want your teenagers to be rooted in Christ, to see the world through a biblical lens because of their intimacy with Christ, and to know what it means to live for Christ in this crazy world, then let me commend *Life with Jesus: Youth Edition*. It is biblically sound, resonates with the issues and questions teenagers experience, and is written in a way to spark meaningful gospel conversations between youth and their leaders."

MIKE MCGARRY, Director, Youth Pastor Theologian;
Author, *A Biblical Theology of Youth Ministry*

"*Life with Jesus: Youth Edition* is a fabulous primer on the Christian life for teens! It's deeply biblical, highly relevant, gospel-centered, and easy for a youth leader (or parent) to pick up and use with their teens. The relatable stories, Scripture reflections, practical teaching, and interactive opening activities make this book perfect for youth groups, small groups, or one-on-one mentoring. Thank you for creating such a valuable youth ministry resource!"

JENNiFER M. KVAMME, Author, *More to the Story*; Student Ministries Catalyst, Centennial Church, Forest Lake, MN

"Another fab resource for young people from The Good Book Company! The shared wisdom of Tim Chester and Katy Morgan make the Bible studies clear, relevant and life-changing—with fun illustrations to keep young minds engaged. The twelve studies provide essential knowledge and practical guidance for healthy growing disciples and can be used by individuals or families or as part of a youth discipleship programme."

NiCK JACKMAN, Director, Contagious Bible Ministries

LIFE WITH JESUS

YOUTH EDITION

thegoodbook
COMPANY

Life with Jesus: Youth Edition
© Tim Chester and Katy Morgan 2025

Published by:
The Good Book Company

thegoodbook.com | thegoodbook.co.uk
thegoodbook.com.au | thegoodbook.co.nz | thegoodbook.co.in

Design by André Parker | Illustrations by Jason Ramasami

ISBN: 9781802541380 | JOB-007874 | Printed in India

CONTENTS

 # iNTRODUCTiON

I don't know what your hopes and dreams for your life are, but I'm guessing that you want it to be *good*. Everyone wants to live life to the full in one way or another—whether that's travelling the world, finding the perfect partner, making millions or just having plenty of time to sit on the sofa and chill.

Did you know that Jesus came to give us life to the full? He said it in John 10 v 10. Jesus promises that when we follow him, we will experience life as it's meant to be lived—because we're connected to the God who made both us and everything around us.

Life with Jesus isn't always straightforward or easy, but it *is* the good life. It's a life of purpose, wisdom and hope, where we get to walk alongside Jesus and learn from him every single day.

That's what this course is all about. We'll talk about who Jesus is, what it looks like to follow him and how he enables us to keep going. Whether you're sure that you're a Christian, you're on the fence or you're new to it all, this is your invitation to explore Jesus' offer of life with him—his offer of life to the full.

HOW iT WORKS

Each session contains four elements:

Meet... A little story to get you thinking about the topic.

Bible Time. A short Bible study that connects with the scenario you just read about.

Think it Through. Two pages of teaching to read, together with a few questions to discuss.

Reflect. Use this space to write a prayer, scribble down key points you want to remember, or anything else. Your leader might give you specific ideas for filling this page in some sessions.

FOR LEADERS

At the back of the book you'll find ideas for games and reflection activities—one each per session. These are primarily designed for youth groups, but most of the reflections will still work if you're using this book in a smaller discipleship meet-up.

Be creative about how you use this book—it'll work best differently in different settings! For example, you could...

- Start with an activity, or put one in the middle of the session to break things up.

- Choose just one part of the **Think it Through** pages (they're always divided into two sections), whichever works best for your group.

- Use the **Think it Through** pages as the basis for a short talk or seminar.

- Perform the **Meet...** section as a drama.

- Do part of the session as one big group, then divide into smaller groups for other parts.

- Ask the young people to do **Bible Time** on their own in advance, then focus on **Think it Through** in the time you have together.

- Turn the course into four super-sessions by combining the chapters into groups of three.

- Add your own questions, games, creative reflection ideas and anything else!

Finally, make sure you leave time to pray—both as leaders and when the group meets. After all, this course on its own will not bring growth in Christ. It is God who makes people more like his Son, through his word and by his Spirit.

PART ONE

PUTTiNG OUT SHOOTS

A new plant needs three things to survive: water, sunlight and nutrients. Christians have some basic needs too. If we're going to start putting out shoots in our life with Jesus, there are three things we need to get straight first of all.

The gospel: why did Jesus come, and why is that good news?

Grace: how do we qualify for this new life with Jesus?

And church: where do we belong, and how do we grow in our faith?

1. JESUS WINS

EXPLORING THE GOSPEL

MEET AVA AND JORDAN

Ava looked at Jordan, sitting next to her in the school cafeteria. It was plain that he was nervous. Very nervous. He kept glancing at her, mouth open, then looking away again.

"What?" she snapped eventually.

Jordan met her eyes at last. "It's just..." he stuttered. "Well, I wanted to tell you." He swallowed. "I've become a Christian."

Ava blinked. This wasn't what she'd expected. "A Christian," she said. "So what does that mean? You going to be all perfect and good now? Get all religious?"

"No..." Jordan answered, frowning. "Don't worry, I'm not going to suddenly be a different person." He paused. "Except, I guess I am a different person now in some ways. It's hard to explain... Christianity isn't just about being good. And it's not just being religious."

Ava raised her eyebrows. "What *is* it about, then?"

★ What would you say if you were Jordan?

BiBLE TiME: COLOSSiANS 1 V 18-23

¹⁸ And he [Jesus] is the head of the body, the church; he

is the beginning and the firstborn from among the dead,

so that in everything he might have the supremacy. ¹⁹ For God was

pleased to have all his fullness dwell in him, ²⁰ and through him to

reconcile to himself all things, whether things on earth or things in

heaven, by making peace through his blood, shed on the cross.

²¹ Once you were alienated from God

and were enemies in your minds because

of your evil behaviour. ²² But now he has

reconciled you by Christ's physical body

through death to present you holy in

his sight, without blemish and free from

accusation— ²³ if you continue in your

faith, established and firm, and do not move from the hope held

out in the gospel. This is the gospel that you heard and that has

been proclaimed to every creature under heaven, and of which I,

Paul, have become a servant.

1. Read Colossians 1 v 18-20. Can you pick out one thing that Jesus *has done*, and two things that Jesus *is*?

2. Read verses 21-23. How does verse 21 describe people before they become Christians?

3. How does verse 22 describe people *after* they become Christians?

4. What has Jesus done to bring about this change? (Look at verses 20 and 22.)

5. Based on this, what do you think Jordan could say to Ava?

DICTIONARY

supremacy = first place
reconcile = bring back together
alienated = separated or far apart
without blemish = perfect

THINK IT THROUGH

VICTORY FOR WHO?

The Christian message is good news—the good news that Jesus has triumphed over evil.

To understand who the winners are in this victory, we need to wind the clock back to the beginning of history. God made a world of beauty and wonder where humans could share his joy. But humanity rejected God's rule. We wanted to be gods of our own lives. We still do. This is what the Bible calls "sin". Our rebellion has put us on a collision course with God.

★ What do you think it means to try to be "gods of our own lives"? Can you think of ways in which people might try to do this, even if they wouldn't express it that way?

Jesus came to defeat evil. That's really good news. Unless you're a rebel against God—and all of us start life as rebels against God. For rebels, Jesus' victory means defeat and judgment.

That's not good.

But the wonderful twist in the story is that we *can* share in Jesus' victory, even though we've rebelled against him. How? Because God's judgment fell upon Jesus himself at the cross. Jesus died under God's judgment in our place so we could go free. Three days later God raised him to life again as the beginning of God's new people and the Lord of God's restored kingdom.

Jesus' victory is good news for sinners!

★ Jesus has already defeated sin and death and, if we follow him, we share in that victory. How could this change life now?

14

WHAT iT'S ALL ABOUT

Here are some assumptions that people make about Christianity.

It's about trying to be good.

It's about believing that God exists.

It's about being religious and going to church.

+ Why might someone making each of those statements assume that Christianity is not for them?

The truth is that first and foremost, Christianity is about Jesus. He has won a victory, and we get to share in it! This means that...

Christianity is not about trying to be good—though it does transform us.

Christianity is not a new set of opinions—though it does make us see many things differently.

Christianity is not becoming religious—though it will make us want to pray.

First and foremost, Christianity is about Jesus, his victory and how we get to share that victory.

+ Is there any way in which you need to reset your own thinking about what Christianity is all about?

+ Is there any way in which faith in Jesus hasn't yet changed your life, but you want it to?

REFLECT

Don't rush off—take some time to reflect on what you've read and discussed. What do you want to remember? How will it affect your week? Use pages like this to write prayers or notes, to doodle, or anything else. You can also find reflection ideas for every chapter at the back of the book.

2. EMPTY HANDS

EXPLORING GRACE

MEET FREYA AND MOLLY

"I'm definitely going to try harder from now on."

It had been Freya's first visit to church. Now she and Molly were walking home together.

"What do you mean?" asked Molly.

"I love it," said Freya. "I love it all. Going to church. Hearing about God. Jesus. A life of love. It all sounds great. So I'm going to try harder. Then maybe I can be a Christian like you."

Molly shook her head. "You can't make yourself a Christian by trying harder. You just need to trust in Jesus."

"What? Surely there's more to it than that. What about loving your neighbour and going to church? Surely they're important. Christians do good, don't they?"

Molly hesitated. How was she going to explain it?

✦ What do you think about what Freya said?

BiBLE TiME: EPHESiANS 2 V 1–10

¹ As for you, you were dead in your transgressions and sins, ² in which you used to live when you followed the ways of this world and of the ruler of the kingdom of the air, the spirit who is now at work in those who are disobedient. ³ All of us also lived among them at one time, gratifying the cravings of our flesh and following its desires and thoughts. Like the rest, we were by nature deserving of wrath.

⁴ But because of his great love for us, God, who is rich in mercy, ⁵ made us alive with Christ even when we were dead in transgressions—it is by grace you have been saved. ⁶ And God raised us up with Christ and seated us with him in the heavenly realms in Christ Jesus, ⁷ in order that in the coming ages he might show the incomparable riches of his grace, expressed in his kindness to us in Christ Jesus.

⁸ For it is by grace you have been saved, through faith—and this is not from yourselves, it is the gift of God— ⁹ not by works, so that no one can boast. ¹⁰ For we are God's handiwork, created in Christ Jesus to do good works, which God prepared in advance for us to do.

1. Read Ephesians 2 v 1-3. What's the situation that all people are in before they become Christians?

2. Read verses 4-7. What has God done? (At least two things.)

3. Read verses 8-10. How do Christians get saved?

4. How do good works fit in to all of this?

5. Based on this, what would you say to Molly and Freya?

DICTIONARY

transgressions = sins
gratifying the cravings of our flesh = doing whatever we felt like
wrath = God's righteous anger

THINK IT THROUGH

EMPTY HANDS

A person becomes a Christian when they respond to the good news by repenting and believing. "Repenting" literally means "turning around"—away from life without God and towards life with God. "Believing" or "faith" means agreeing with the message, but also entrusting yourself to Jesus as your Saviour.

It is like holding out empty hands to God. We don't say, "Look at my good works, my religious activity, my respectable life". Instead our hands are empty to receive salvation as a gift.

After all, human beings are too messed up to be able to earn anything from God. We were a bit like zombies—dead souls walking about in living bodies (Ephesians 2 v 1). We couldn't please God. We may well have done plenty of good things. But the basic direction of our lives was away from God.

Fortunately, God didn't wait for us to make the first move. He took the initiative when he sent Jesus.

We don't get God's blessing because we do good things. We are acceptable to God because Jesus died on our behalf.

★ Why do you think people might sometimes find it hard to accept that they can't be good enough for God on their own?

★ If you think your relationship with God depends on good works, what's likely to happen when you have a bad day? How does being saved by grace change this?

20

WHERE GOOD WORKS FIT IN

Ephesians 2 v 10 tells us that Jesus saved us "to do good works, which God prepared in advance for us to do". We already know that good works don't save us. But God *does* give us good works to do.

Think of it like this. Apples don't give life to a branch. But they are a sign that a branch has life. Life comes first and then apples.

In the same way, good works don't *make* us spiritually alive, but they are the *fruit* of genuine spiritual life. Good works don't create our relationship with God, but they may help us enjoy that relationship.

It's Jesus who connects us to God, and that connection can't be any stronger than it already is.

★ How could all of this change the way we view ourselves...

... when we've just done something really nice for someone?

... when we've just done something really terrible to someone?

... when we feel like God couldn't love us because we're so bad?

... when we feel like *of course* God loves us because we're great?

REFLECT

3. PART OF THE FAMILY

EXPLORING CHURCH

MEET MAX AND ROHAN

It was late on Friday night. Max slumped on the sofa, got out his phone and texted Rohan. *Hey, you ok? Missed you at church.*

Max didn't have to wait long for Rohan's reply. *Yeah sorry. I was just really tired.*

Tell me about it, wrote Max. Then wondered what to say next. But Rohan was typing.

To be honest I'm not sure about church right now, came the message a few minutes later. *I want to be a Christian and everything. But I've got nothing in common with people at church. Do I really have to go?*

Max bit his lip as he looked at his phone. Normally he'd have been straight in there with an answer. But the truth was, it was a question he'd been asking himself too. Church could be hard work sometimes.

His thumb hovered over the screen. What was he going to say?

✦ What do you think Max should reply?

BiBLE TiME: COLOSSiANS 3 V 7-17

[7] You used to walk in these ways, in the life you once lived. [8] But now you must also rid yourselves of all such things as these: anger, rage, malice, slander, and filthy language from your lips. [9] Do not lie to each other, since you have taken off your old self with its practices [10] and have put on the new self, which is being renewed in knowledge in the image of its Creator. [11] Here there is no Gentile or Jew, circumcised or uncircumcised, barbarian, Scythian, slave or free, but Christ is all, and is in all.

[12] Therefore, as God's chosen people, holy and dearly loved, clothe yourselves with compassion, kindness, humility, gentleness and patience. [13] Bear with each other and forgive one another if any of you has a grievance against someone. Forgive as the Lord forgave you. [14] And over all these virtues put on love, which binds them all together in perfect unity.

[15] Let the peace of Christ rule in your hearts, since as members of one body you were called to peace. And be thankful.

[16] Let the message of Christ dwell among you richly as you teach and admonish one another with all wisdom through psalms, hymns, and songs from the Spirit, singing to God with gratitude in your hearts. [17] And whatever you do, whether in word or deed, do it all in the name of the Lord Jesus, giving thanks to God the Father through him.

1. Read Colossians 3 v 7-11. What are the "old self" and the "new self"?

2. Read verses 12-15. How should our "new self" affect our relationships with other Christians?

3. Read verses 16-17. How do we help each other to grow as Christians, according to these verses?

4. What's the link between being your "new self" and being together with other Christians?

5. What would you say to Max and Rohan about all of this?

DICTIONARY

malice = evil thoughts about someone else
slander = lying about someone else
Gentile = non-Jewish person
grievance = complaint
admonish = warn

THINK IT THROUGH

PART OF THE FAMILY

How do you spot someone who supports a particular sports team? Fans express their allegiance by wearing the colours of their team. Paul uses a similar image to describe what happens when someone becomes a Christian. We take off the "old self" like an old football shirt, and put on the "new self" instead.

Our "old self" basically causes conflict. Human beings were made to live in relationship with God and one another, but sin messed that up in a big way. That's why our world is so full of divisions—groups of people that just can't get along with each other.

But our "new self" is different. In the church, through Christ, our humanity is being restored. The differences between us no longer have to divide us, because Jesus has united us.

+ What differences can you think of that divide people today?

+ Why does it change the way we relate to each other if Christ has made us new?

Paul calls us "God's chosen people, holy and dearly loved" (v 12). The Bible story is not simply the story of how God saves *individuals*. It's the story of God's *people*. We're saved into a shared life. Paul describes us as "members of one body" (v 15). It doesn't really matter whether you see yourself as a hand, an ear or a little toe—the point is, what unites us is more important than what divides us. We belong together and we need one another.

GROWING TOGETHER

Paul is realistic. He knows that life in a local church can sometimes feel a bit boring—or the opposite, full of arguments! This is why he mixes grand descriptions of who we are in Christ with encouragements to put that reality into practice. The way we treat each other matters—it's how we display Jesus' love and peace.

> ✦ How do people at your church relate to one another? How different is it to the way non-Christians relate to one another?

Church isn't always perfect. But it is God's gift to you to help you grow. Think of yourself as a piece of coal on fire for Jesus. In the middle of a fireplace, surrounded by other blazing coals, a piece of coal happily remains red hot. But take a piece of coal out of the fire and it soon loses its heat. It's the same with Christians. Take a Christian out of a local church for any length of time and they're likely to lose their passion—the fire goes out. But in the midst of a living church, our passion for Jesus is much more likely to remain red hot.

So, there are two reasons to be part of a local church. First, there's the identity reason. You've been saved into the community of Christ. This is who we are—the family of God. Second, there's the practical reason. Your church has been given to you by Christ as the place where you can survive and thrive as a Christian.

> ✦ In what ways has church helped you to thrive?

> ✦ What could you do to help others to thrive?

REFLECT

PART TWO

SEEiNG THiNGS DiFFERENTLY

Life with Jesus is a bit like getting new glasses. You start seeing things differently. In this part of the book we're going to see how Jesus changes the way we approach the fundamentals of life.

Obedience: how does our relationship with God affect our behaviour?

Union with Christ: how does Jesus empower us to keep going?

And suffering: what difference does Jesus make when life gets tough?

4. CHILDREN, NOT SLAVES

EXPLORING OBEDIENCE

MEET JACK AND OLLY

Jack had stopped swearing pretty much overnight and he was doing his best to be nicer to his mother. There was no doubt that becoming a Christian had changed his life. But anger was still a big issue. He still found it tough not to let his emotions spiral out of control.

How could he pray and all that when he was such a rubbish Christian?

His friend Ollie said, "It's all about what Jesus has done for us, isn't it? It doesn't matter what we do. God isn't a slave-driver. Just chill out a bit."

Jack wasn't sure. Okay, maybe God *was* more patient than Jack had given him credit for. But you weren't really a Christian if you just didn't bother obeying, were you?

✱ Who do you think is right, Ollie or Jack? Have you ever thought something similar to either of them?

BiBLE TiME: ROMANS 8 V 12-16

12 Therefore, brothers and sisters, we have an

obligation—but it is not to the flesh, to live according to

it. 13 For if you live according to the flesh, you will die; but if by the

Spirit you put to death the misdeeds of the body, you will live.

14 For those who are led by the Spirit of God are the children of God.
15 The Spirit you received does not make you slaves, so that you

live in fear again; rather, the Spirit you received brought about your

adoption to sonship. And by him we cry, "Abba, Father." 16 The Spirit

himself testifies with our spirit that we are God's children.

1. Read Romans 8 v 12-13. What do you think it means to "live according to the flesh"? And what's the opposite way of living?

2. How does this back up what Jack was saying?

3. Read verses 14-16. How do these verses describe our relationship with God?

4. Underline everything the Spirit does in these verses. How does he change the way we view God?

5. How does this back up what Ollie was saying?

” DiCTiONARY

obligation = something you have to do
the flesh = your sinful self
Abba = Dad
testifies = declares

THINK IT THROUGH

A GOOD FATHER

Nothing matters more than the way you think about God. If you think of God as a tyrant, then you'll keep him at arm's length or you'll feel like a slave. God doesn't want us to live like that, so he sent his Spirit to help us recognise that he is actually a Father. And not a cold, distant, selfish father, but a close, loving, generous father—the best father! Jesus is God's child by nature, and if we believe in him then we become God's children by adoption. It's so amazing that we would never believe it if the Spirit didn't help us!

> ★ What's the difference between a slave obeying a master and a child obeying a father?

God's rule is a rule of love. His first words to humanity were: "You are free". "You are free to eat from any tree in the garden; but you must not eat from the tree of the knowledge of good and evil" (Genesis 2 v 16-17). That one restriction gave humanity an opportunity to trust God.

We often assume that freedom involves having lots of choices. But true freedom is the capacity to be the best you can be and enjoy what's best for you. Freedom for a fish is not the choice to jump out of the water—that's not freedom, but death. That's because fish thrive in water. Likewise, freedom for human beings is not the choice to be bad—that's not true freedom, but slavery and death. That's because human beings thrive under God's rule of love. God's law isn't a cage, hemming us in. It is more like a skeleton, holding us up.

> ★ Can you think of any times when you've been tempted to sin but you haven't? Why was it good to obey God in those situations?

A RUTHLESS FIGHT

Romans 8 v 12-13 say that we now have "an obligation": to "put to death the misdeeds of the body". This means ruthlessly saying no to temptation. We fight temptation through faith in the truth that God is our good Father. Take Jack's struggle with anger. Imagine a friend lets Jack down in a project they were supposed to do together at school. Now Jack is about to blow. How can he fight temptation?

✦ Here are some reasons why Jack might be angry, and some truths he could fight temptation with. Can you match them up?

Jack is angry because he likes being in control.	Jack is a child of God, so he doesn't need to find his identity in his work.
Jack is angry because his teacher will blame him.	God is in control, and we can trust him to do what's best for us.
Jack is angry because his academic record will now be ruined.	God's opinion is the only opinion that really matters.

Obeying God can be tough. It goes against the grain of our old sinful instincts. It can put us out of step with everyone around us.

But if we're ever tempted to doubt the goodness of God, we just need to think of Jesus. The cross is the great demonstration that God's intentions for us are good—which means that obeying him will lead to a satisfying life. Remembering this truth helps us say no to temptation. Never forget that we fight temptation *by the Spirit*. God gives us his Spirit to empower us and inspire us, and to remind us of his fatherly love.

REFLECT

5. ROOT AND BRANCH
EXPLORING OUR UNION WITH CHRIST

MEET NARMA

Narma had been so excited when she'd first become a Christian. It was amazing to think of God as her Father. She loved praying. And she loved discovering one amazing thing after another when she read her Bible. She wanted to tell everyone she met about Jesus.

But she soon discovered that people weren't always interested in listening. Even her Christian friends had got a bit fed up. What was new to her wasn't new to them. Then she moved to a school further away and that meant less time to read her Bible in the morning. She tried reading on the bus, but it was hard to concentrate.

Today she'd got home from school and realised it was youth group night. Her heart sank. All she wanted to do was slump on the sofa and watch TV.

"How's it going?" asked one of the leaders when she got to church.

"I don't know," said Narma. There was a pause. Then she asked, "Why does being a Christian suddenly feel like such hard work?"

+ What would you say to Narma?

BiBLE TiME: JOHN 15 V 4–14

4 "Remain in me, as I also remain in you. No branch can bear fruit by itself; it must remain in the vine. Neither can you bear fruit unless you remain in me.

5 "I am the vine; you are the branches. If you remain in me and I in you, you will bear much fruit; apart from me you can do nothing. 6 If you do not remain in me, you are like a branch that is thrown away and withers; such branches are picked up, thrown into the fire and burned. 7 If you remain in me and my words remain in you, ask whatever you wish, and it will be done for you. 8 This is to my Father's glory, that you bear much fruit, showing yourselves to be my disciples.

9 "As the Father has loved me, so have I loved you. Now remain in my love. 10 If you keep my commands, you will remain in my love, just as I have kept my Father's commands and remain in his love. 11 I have told you this so that my joy may be in you and that your joy may be complete. 12 My command is this: love each other as I have loved you. 13 Greater love has no one than this: to lay down one's life for one's friends. 14 You are my friends if you do what I command."

1. Read John 15 v 4-8. This is Jesus speaking to his disciples. What does he mean when he says he's like a vine and we're like branches?

2. In the same verses, underline all the times Jesus uses the phrase "remain in me". What will happen if we remain in Jesus?

3. Read verses 9-14. What does it actually mean to remain in Jesus?

4. What does Jesus say that he does or will do?

5. What does Narma need to do in order to keep on keeping Jesus' commands?

THINK IT THROUGH

CONNECTED

What's the secret to being a successful Christian? Jesus said, "Remain in me, as I also remain in you." When you become a Christian, you're united to Christ, like branches in a vine. But what does it mean to be "in Christ" and to "remain in Christ"? Well, Jesus calls his disciples friends (v 14). To remain in Christ is to remain friends with him.

> ✦ How do you remain friends with someone? What do you have to do?

Being in Christ is a connection made by the Holy Spirit—a connection that's living and life-giving. Just as life flows from a vine to its branches, so life flows from Christ to us through the Holy Spirit. And just like a branch connected to a vine, this connection to Jesus means we bear fruit. For Christians that means "love, joy, peace, forbearance, kindness, goodness, faithfulness, gentleness and self-control" (Galatians 5 v 22-23).

Think of it like this. Most of us have relationships we find energising. When we spend time with these people, we come away feeling buoyed up or inspired. Our relationship with Jesus is a super-energising relationship. Spending time with him inspires us or reassures us or excites us. That's partly because he's such an inspirational person. But it's also because our connection with him is supernatural. Jesus is full of life! Some of that life flows to us when we spend time with him.

> ✦ What ways can you think of to "spend time with Jesus"?

THE HOW-TO

How do we remain connected to Jesus? Look back at the passage we read earlier and fill in the gaps.

* *We listen to what Jesus says.* Verse 7 says Jesus' _____ need to remain in us. This means we _____ to Jesus by hearing from the _____.

* *We ask for what Jesus offers.* Jesus promises to give us _____ (v 7). Verse 8 helps us understand that what he means is things that will bring _____ to the Father.

* *We love what Jesus loves.* In verse 12 Jesus commands us to _____.

Following Jesus can be hard going. Reading the Bible takes time and sometimes we'd rather do something else. Loving other people often involves sacrifice. If we neglect our relationship with Jesus, then being a Christian can feel like a bunch of obligations. Then it becomes a slog. What energises us is our connection to Jesus. So when service feels like a burden, it's time to reconnect with Jesus.

"I have told you this," says Jesus, "so that my joy may be in you and that your joy may be complete" (v 11).

* When have you personally felt most connected to Jesus?

REFLECT

6. HOPE AND GLORY

EXPLORING SUFFERING

MEET HANNAH AND JOE

Joe and Hannah were sitting in their favourite fried chicken restaurant. Hannah kept picking at her fries, not eating much. Joe could see that something was wrong.

"Do you want to talk about it?" he asked.

Hannah hesitated. "It's my sister. She's so ill. I've asked God to cure her again and again, but nothing's happened. I thought Jesus healed people. I don't get why he won't heal her. Maybe he doesn't love her."

Joe was trying to work out what to say when Hannah continued. "I saw this thing on YouTube that said we sometimes don't get what we want because we don't have enough faith. Do you think that's true? Maybe it's my fault my sister's not getting better." She shook her head. "I don't know what to think."

+ What would you say to Hannah?

BIBLE TIME: ROMANS 8 V 18-23, 26-28

18 I consider that our present sufferings are not worth comparing with the glory that will be revealed in us. 19 For the creation waits in eager expectation for the children of God to be revealed. 20 For the creation was subjected to frustration, not by its own choice, but by the will of the one who subjected it, in hope 21 that the creation itself will be liberated from its bondage to decay and brought into the freedom and glory of the children of God.

22 We know that the whole creation has been groaning as in the pains of childbirth right up to the present time. 23 Not only so, but we ourselves, who have the firstfruits of the Spirit, groan inwardly as we wait eagerly for our adoption to sonship, the redemption of our bodies. ...

26 In the same way, the Spirit helps us in our weakness. We do not know what we ought to pray for, but the Spirit himself intercedes for us through wordless groans. 27 And he who searches our hearts knows the mind of the Spirit, because the Spirit intercedes for God's people in accordance with the will of God. 28 And we know that in all things God works for the good of those who love him, who have been called according to his purpose.

1. Read Romans 8 v 19-21 slowly. What is the world like now, and what will happen to it in the future? Underline phrases that help you with the first question, and circle phrases that help you with the second.

2. Read verses 18 and 22-23. What's the experience of Christians now, and what will be our experience in the future? Underline phrases that help you with the first question, and circle phrases that help you with the second.

3. Read verses 26-27. What is the Holy Spirit doing when we find life tough?

4. Read verse 28. Why might these words encourage Hannah?

" DICTIONARY

subjected to frustration = held back from the way it should be
we ... have the firstfruits of the Spirit = we have the Spirit already, but one day we'll be blessed even more
intercedes = prays

THINK IT THROUGH

A NEW HOPE

Christianity is the good news of the victory of Jesus. So why is life often tough? Where's the victory when someone loses their job or is diagnosed with cancer?

The answer is that God is waiting before he restores creation. He's waiting so that people have the opportunity to turn to him in faith and repentance. In the meantime, Romans 8 gives us three wonderful truths that help us cope when suffering comes our way.

God will end suffering: One day God will renew all things and there will be no more sickness, suffering, sin or death.

God is with us in our suffering: God the Son has experienced what it is to be human. Jesus knows what it's like to be weary, frustrated, bereaved, misunderstood and betrayed. And now his Spirit "helps us in our weakness" (v 26).

God uses suffering to make us like Jesus: God uses "all things"—including suffering—for our good (v 28). Suffering deepens our character, makes us depend more on Jesus, and focuses our attention on eternal glory. We can't always see how this process is happening, but we can be confident that God's purposes for us are good because he's given us his Son.

✦ Why might each of those truths help someone who is suffering?

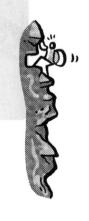

SUFFERING AND THEN GLORY

Some Christians expect God to make them healthy and wealthy here and now. But the Bible says we're not there yet. The world has not yet been made new. In the meantime, we must be patient.

Christians are not immune to suffering. We're not like someone on a mountain ski lift gliding past people struggling with walking poles and rough terrain. That's not real life, and it's not what God promises.

The truth is that we're following the pattern of Jesus himself. He suffered, and then he was raised to life. Likewise, we will suffer in one way or another here on earth—but one day all our suffering will end and we will be part of a glorious new creation.

In the meantime, we're not left on our own. We have the Holy Spirit to connect us with Jesus and help us to live for him. Romans 8 v 37-39 tells us that nothing—*nothing*—can separate us from God's love.

★ In light of all of this, what would you say to someone who claims we can be healed if we just have enough faith?

★ What would you say to someone who says that suffering is a sign that God doesn't really love us?

★ What's one thing you want to remember from this session for the next time you find life really hard?

REFLECT

PART THREE

CONNECTING WITH GOD

Ever had a friendship with someone you'd never seen, heard from, or connected with in any way? It wouldn't be much of a friendship. Relationships require connection. We can't see God, but that doesn't mean he doesn't show us his love. That's what we're talking about in this section.

The Bible: how does God speak?

Prayer: how do we speak back?

And communion: how do we really *experience* God's love?

7. GOD SPEAKS

EXPLORING THE BIBLE

MEET SOPHIE AND CHLOE

"Why on *earth* are you reading that?"

Sophie looked up guiltily as her sister came into their bedroom. She'd been reading the Bible—starting with Mark's Gospel, like the pastor at church had said. She'd been trying to get into the habit of it, but it was hard when she shared a room with Chloe.

"The Bible's *boring*," declared Chloe as she flopped on her bed. "And old-fashioned. And just plain old. You're wasting your time."

"It... it's important," answered Sophie. But the truth was, she wasn't sure what to say. She knew the Bible was God's word, but it was confusing sometimes. On Sundays, when the pastor preached, it all made sense. But on her own at home, it was sometimes hard to see what relevance it had to her.

She looked down at the page in front of her, feeling embarrassed. Why *was* she bothering to read the Bible?

★ What would you say to Sophie or Chloe?

BIBLE TIME: 2 PETER 1 V 12, 16–21

¹² So I will always remind you of these things, even though you know them and are firmly established in the truth you now have. ...

¹⁶ For we did not follow cleverly devised stories when we told you about the coming of our Lord Jesus Christ in power, but we were eye-witnesses of his majesty. ¹⁷ He received honour and glory from God the Father when the voice came to him from the Majestic Glory, saying, 'This is my Son, whom I love; with him I am well pleased.' ¹⁸ We ourselves heard this voice that came from heaven when we were with him on the sacred mountain.

¹⁹ We also have the prophetic message as something completely reliable, and you will do well to pay attention to it, as to a light shining in a dark place, until the day dawns and the morning star rises in your hearts. ²⁰ Above all, you must understand that no prophecy of Scripture came about by the prophet's own interpretation of things. ²¹ For prophecy never had its origin in the human will, but prophets, though human, spoke from God as they were carried along by the Holy Spirit.

1. Read 2 Peter 1 v 16-18. Where did Peter get the stories about Jesus which he and others passed on (and which became the New Testament)?

2. Read verses 19-21. Here Peter is talking about the prophets who wrote the Old Testament. What do you think he most wants us to know about the Old Testament?

3. What was the relationship between the human authors and the Holy Spirit in the writing of the Bible?

4. Read verse 12 and look again at verse 19. What difference does Peter say the Old and New Testaments can make to his readers?

5. How does this start to answer some of Chloe and Sophie's doubts?

 ## DICTIONARY

firmly established = securely set up

devised = invented

the prophetic message = the Old Testament

THiNK iT THROUGH

A WORD FROM THE LORD

Imagine someone providing you with nourishing meals day after day. They do all the hard work, but you still need to eat the food. Those meals won't do you any good if the food stays on the plate. In the same way, if we want to grow as Christians, we need to use the gifts which Jesus has given us for that purpose. The first one we're going to look at is his word, the Bible.

Peter wants us to be clear that we can absolutely trust what's written in the Bible. The Bible is the word of God because the Spirit of God ensured that what was written was exactly what God intended. Every part of the Bible has two authors. There's the human author with their own distinctive style and personality. But there's also the divine author. So we read the words of Moses or David or Isaiah or Peter, but at the same time they're also the words of God. That means what we read is "completely reliable" (v 19). The Bible is true and trustworthy.

★ The Bible was written by human authors to particular people facing particular challenges. How might that affect the way we read it?

★ The Bible was also written by God! How should that affect the way we read it?

★ Why does it matter that the Bible is trustworthy?

A WORD FOR YOU AND ME

✦ Complete each heading below by choosing one of the following words: *Christ-centred / life-giving / loving / relevant*

1. A _____ book

The Spirit spoke through the *writers* of the Bible, and he continues to speak to *readers* of the Bible. It is through God's word that the Holy Spirit keeps us going—giving life to our hearts.

2. A _____ book

The Bible was written *for you*. Most books of the Bible were first written for a specific situation, so it helps to keep the original readers in mind. But the Bible always works beyond its original context. It is written to help you endure, to encourage you and to give you hope.

3. A _____ book

When the relevance to you is hard to spot, remember that the Bible is all about Jesus. That's fairly obvious in the New Testament. But the Old Testament, too, is full of promises and pictures of Jesus.

4. A _____ book

Above all, what we hear in the Bible are words of love from our Saviour. A lot of the time we're being reminded of what we already know—just like a child hearing words of reassurance from their parents. Christ speaks words of comfort to our battered hearts and words of life to our weary souls.

✦ Peter describes God's word as like "a light shining in a dark place". Why do you think he said that? Does it seem that way to you?

REFLECT

8. A FATHER WHO LISTENS

EXPLORING PRAYER

MEET MO AND CARL

Small-group time had ended and once again Mo had just frozen when it was time to pray.

"You don't need to worry," said the leader, Carl. "It's just talking to God."

"It's embarrassing," groaned Mo. "I'm not like you—you always say such impressive prayers. It's like God's right in front of you. I can't do that. I can't get the words right."

Carl pulled a face. He wasn't such a great pray-er himself, not really. Out loud was much easier—he could say the right words. But when he tried to pray alone at home he just got distracted.

"I don't know if it's really about getting the words right," said Carl. He shook his head, confused suddenly. What *was* the most important thing when it came to prayer?

+ What would you say to Mo? What would you say to Carl?

BIBLE TIME: MATTHEW 6 V 5-13

⁵ And when you pray, do not be like the hypocrites, for they love to pray standing in the synagogues and on the street corners to be seen by others. Truly I tell you, they have received their reward in full. ⁶ But when you pray, go into your room, close the door and pray to your Father, who is unseen. Then your Father, who sees what is done in secret, will reward you. ⁷ And when you pray, do not keep on babbling like pagans, for they think they will be heard because of their many words. ⁸ Do not be like them, for your Father knows what you need before you ask him.

⁹ This, then, is how you should pray:

"Our Father in heaven,

hallowed be your name,

¹⁰ your kingdom come,

your will be done,

on earth as it is in heaven.

¹¹ Give us today our daily bread.

¹² And forgive us our debts,

as we also have forgiven our debtors.

¹³ And lead us not into temptation,

but deliver us from the evil one."

1. Read Matthew 6 v 5-6. This is Jesus speaking to his disciples. What do we learn about God here?

2. How does this affect how we should and shouldn't pray?

3. Read verses 7-8. What do we learn about God here? How does this affect how we should and shouldn't pray?

4. Read verses 9-13. Which bits of this prayer match the types of thing you normally pray about? Which don't so much?

5. Based on all of this, what would you say to Mo and Carl? What is prayer all about?

THiNK iT THROUGH

GETTiNG iT RiGHT

The passage we just read is Jesus' prayer manual, and it boils down to one simple principle: remember that God is your Father.

We're not supposed to pray just to impress other people. Other people might be impressed, it's true—but then that's all the reward we get. Christians come as children to our Father, so our prayers don't have to be impressive. We're also not supposed to try to manipulate God. God is too powerful for nagging to work. But he's also too loving to *need* to be nagged. He's a loving Father who knows what we need before we ask.

What's the technique that will make our prayers effective? There isn't one! That's the point. What counts are not the words you use or how long you pray. What counts is the love of your heavenly Father!

✦ What are some reasons why people might struggle with prayer? How would this passage help with those things?

A MODEL PRAYER

The Lord's Prayer is a kind of model that we can use to shape our own prayers.

Our Father in heaven: Just as Jesus is God's child by nature, so his followers are now God's children by grace. That means Christians share the same access to God that Jesus himself enjoys.

Hallowed be your name: "Hallow" is an old word for "holy". So to pray "hallowed be your name" is to pray for God's reputation—to pray for people to know that he is holy. For example, we could ask for help to reflect God's holiness in the way we live. Or we could ask for people to be saved so that they start honouring God's name.

Your kingdom come: God's kingdom is growing as his word is proclaimed and people submit to him in faith. And one day God's kingdom will be the only show in town. So we pray that we would obey God more, that other people would become Christians, and that Christ would return in victory

Your will be done, on earth as it is in heaven: Jesus prayed these words on the night before he died (Matthew 26 v 42). He felt scared of the cross, but in love he submitted to God's plan. So to pray "your will be done" is to submit to whatever God has chosen for us.

★ How do you think praying prayers like these could affect your life?

Give us today our daily bread: "Daily bread" means all the things we need. Jesus invites us to bring our worries and needs to God so we can focus on serving him.

Forgive us our debts, as we also have forgiven our debtors: By "debts" Jesus means our sins. We owe God love and obedience, but we don't always give him those things—yet God forgives us those debts. Confessing our sins can't change the way God sees us—we've already been forgiven. But it does restore our sense of closeness to God. It also reminds us that God's mercy to us is meant to flow out in mercy towards others.

Lead us not into temptation, but deliver us from evil: The word "temptation" here means both being drawn towards sin and being tested by difficult circumstances. This is not a request to escape temptation but a request that we'll be kept safe through it. We're asking God to help us keep obeying and trusting Jesus, even when it's tough.

★ What's one way that you can imitate Jesus' model prayer (that you don't do already)?

REFLECT

9. GiVE ME A SiGN
EXPLORiNG COMMUNiON

MEET LAiLA

Laila slumped on the sofa. "I just wish I knew for certain Jesus was really there," she muttered, hiding her face in her hands.

She felt the sofa sag as Dad sat down next to her. "Has something happened?" he asked.

"I've just had an awful day," Laila said quietly. "I got a detention. And it was my fault really. I shouted at Mr Wallace." She peeked at Dad through her hands. "Everyone says Jesus forgives you, but what if he doesn't? And why does he let me get angry if he's supposed to be right beside me?" She hid her face again and spoke in a mumble. "I don't think he even loves me. I wish I had some sort of sign."

Laila felt Dad put his arms around her. "Poor Laila," he said. "I don't think Jesus really gives signs." He paused. "But, um, how about a cookie? I've just baked them. It's a sign of MY love at least?"

> ✦ What would you say to Laila? Do you think her dad is right?

BIBLE TIME:
1 CORINTHIANS 10 V 16–17 AND 11 V 23–26

^{10 v 16} Is not the cup of thanksgiving for which we give thanks a participation in the blood of Christ? And is not the bread that we break a participation in the body of Christ? ¹⁷ Because there is one loaf, we, who are many, are one body, for we all share the one loaf. ...

^{11 v 23} For I received from the Lord what I also passed on to you: the Lord Jesus, on the night he was betrayed, took bread, ²⁴ and when he had given thanks, he broke it and said, "This is my body, which is for you; do this in remembrance of me." ²⁵ In the same way, after supper he took the cup, saying, "This cup is the new covenant in my blood; do this, whenever you drink it, in remembrance of me." ²⁶ For whenever you eat this bread and drink this cup, you proclaim the Lord's death until he comes.

1. Read 1 Corinthians 11 v 23-26. Paul is writing about what we call "Communion" or "the Lord's Supper". What do the bread and wine represent? (Underline the relevant bits in the passage.)

2. What are we doing when we eat the bread and drink the wine? (Two things.)

3. Read 10 v 16-17. What do the bread and wine tell us about our relationships with Jesus and with each other?

4. Taking all of that together, what impact do you think the Lord's Supper is supposed to have on those who take it?

5. Why might all of this be helpful for Laila?

 ## DiCTiONARY

participation = taking part
covenant = a kind of contract with God

THINK IT THROUGH
THE PROMISE OF CHRIST

✦ What might you do to remind someone that you love them?

Communion is a memory aid. Of course, it's not that we've forgotten who Jesus is or what he's done. But we easily get distracted. Sometimes all we can see are our problems. Maybe we feel we've let God down and we wonder if he still accepts us. Maybe we are starting to doubt whether Jesus is there at all. Communion helps us take a step back and see the bigger picture. And what we see is God's love displayed in the gift of his Son. Communion is Christ's gift to remind us that he's forgiven all our sins.

✦ Does that resonate with you? When do you need a reminder of Jesus' forgiveness and love?

Jesus could have just given us some words by which to remember him. He could have said, *Say this in remembrance of me*, or *Think this...* But he knows how battered by life we can be. So he gives us a physical sign of his love. We see and taste the promises of Jesus in the bread and wine.

Jesus promises "the forgiveness of sins". But he doesn't just promise this—he makes a covenant. This is a kind of legal contract. Today, you have to sign the bottom of a contract to confirm your commitment to it. The wine of Communion is Jesus' signature! Every time someone receives the Communion wine, Jesus is affirming afresh his commitment to forgive their sins.

THE PRESENCE OF CHRIST

The bread and wine are also signs of Christ's presence. Of course God is present everywhere. But throughout the Bible, God promises to be with his people in a special way—to comfort, guide and protect them. We particularly experience this presence when we gather together as God's people—and above all in Communion.

Paul describes it as "the Lord's table" (1 Corinthians 10 v 21). It's like a dinner party, with Jesus himself as the host. He invites us to eat with him as a sign of his love.

The bread and wine don't literally transform into the physical body and blood of Jesus. Jesus is truly human with a real human body, and he is now in heaven. But although Jesus isn't physically present in his body, he is spiritually present through the Holy Spirit. Not only that; the presence of Jesus takes tangible form in the bread and wine, which represent his body and blood.

Do you ever long for a sign that Jesus is there for you? Bread and wine are that sign. Good parents tell their children that they love them—and so does Jesus in the Bible. But a good parent also hugs their children as a physical demonstration of their commitment to them. Communion is Christ's reassuring hug.

★ What would you say to Laila now?

★ Many churches don't allow younger people to take the bread and wine. If that's you, what do you think you should do while Communion is happening?

REFLECT

PART FOUR

LIVING IT OUT

Life doesn't just happen inside your head. It happens as you go about your day—talking to people, going places, shopping, studying, working… And Jesus wants us to live every part of that life with him by our side. So, how do we do it? We're going to focus on three big areas of life.

Money: what does God say about what we should value?

Romance & sex: what does God say about dating and our bodies?

And evangelism: how does God use our lives and our words to speak to others?

10. TREASURE HUNT

EXPLORING MONEY

MEET RIO AND DAN

It was Tuesday night. Rio loved playing football but, as he and the rest of the team headed onto the field, he noticed yet again that he had the oldest clothes of anyone. To make matters worse, his cousin Dan was telling anyone who would listen about the new phone that his dad had just bought him.

Rio dragged his feet in the mud. "It's not fair," he muttered.

But Dan heard him.

"You jealous?" he mocked. "I thought you were supposed to be a goody-goody Christian. What would Jesus say about being jealous of some stupid phone, huh?"

Rio flushed. "That has nothing to do with it," he said. But he wasn't sure if that was true or not. He'd give practically anything to have the things Dan had. Was that wrong?

★ What advice would you give to Rio?

BiBLE TiME: MATTHEW 6 V 19-24

19 "Do not store up for yourselves treasures on earth, where moths and vermin destroy, and where thieves break in and steal. 20 But store up for yourselves treasures in heaven, where moths and vermin do not destroy, and where thieves do not break in and steal. 21 For where your treasure is, there your heart will be also.

22 "The eye is the lamp of the body. If your eyes are healthy, your whole body will be full of light. 23 But if your eyes are unhealthy, your whole body will be full of darkness. If then the light within you is darkness, how great is that darkness!

24 "No one can serve two masters. Either you will hate the one and love the other, or you will be devoted to the one and despise the other. You cannot serve both God and Money."

1. Read Matthew 6 v 19-21. What do you think Jesus means by "storing up treasures" on earth or in heaven?

2. Why is it better to store up treasures in heaven?

3. Read verses 22-23. Jesus is saying that what we look at will shape our priorities. What do you look at that makes you want to store up treasure on earth? What do you look at that makes you want to store up treasure in heaven?

4. Read verse 24. What do you think it looks like to serve money?

5. What would you say to Rio about all of this?

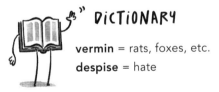 DiCTiONARY

vermin = rats, foxes, etc.
despise = hate

THINK IT THROUGH

THE GREATEST TREASURE

Jesus once told a story about a man who found some treasure in a field. The man sold everything he owned to buy the field and enjoy the treasure (Matthew 13 v 44). People must have thought the man was crazy—selling everything to buy a scrappy piece of land. But Jesus says he did so "in his joy". Of course he did: he was getting something much more valuable!

Christians have found an amazing treasure. We've found forgiveness, freedom and eternal life. Above all, we've found Jesus. And so, in our joy we make sacrifices to follow Jesus—because he's worth more than anything else.

> ✦ If Jesus is someone's highest treasure, how would that affect the way they make decisions and the things they prioritise?

"If only I had more money," many people think, "then I would be happy." But it doesn't work, because we were made for more—we were made for God. And in the end you can't take money with you. So Jesus tells us to store up treasure in heaven rather than on earth.

We know it makes sense. But money still has a powerful pull on our hearts. Jesus says that we can't serve two masters. There's nothing wrong with money itself—it can do a lot of good. But money can be like a god. We think it will rescue us from our problems and make us happy. So we make sacrifices for it. This is what makes it so dangerous. It can become a rival to Jesus in our lives.

> ✦ Can you think of some ways in which money might become the "god" of someone your age?

GRATEFUL AND GENEROUS

Instead of pursuing wealth, we're to pursue contentment. But how can we find contentment? One simple thing we can do is to be grateful. It's easy to focus on what we lack. We imagine that if only we could buy those shoes, go to that game, redecorate our room, then we'd be happy. But all the time, God has blessed us in a thousand wonderful ways. The act of giving thanks redirects our thinking from what we lack to what we've received, and from the gift to the Giver.

> ✦ Do you think that a poor person can be just as grateful as a rich person? Why or why not?

God also encourages us to be generous with our money, time, homes and possessions. Giving money is an important way to support Christian work and care for those in need. But it also benefits *us*: being generous liberates us from the power of money and helps us appreciate the generosity of God.

Back in the Old Testament, the people of Israel were encouraged to give a tenth of their income to the temple (i.e. to God's work). There's no rule for Christians today. Instead, our standard is the jaw-dropping generosity of Jesus. The apostle Paul wrote:

"See that you also excel in this grace of giving ... For you know the grace of our Lord Jesus Christ, that though he was rich, yet for your sake he became poor, so that you through his poverty might become rich." (2 Corinthians 8 v 7, 9)

> ✦ How can we help ourselves to grow in generosity?

REFLECT

11. TRUE LOVE

EXPLORING ROMANCE*

MEET TiA AND MARiE

Tia and Marie were sitting in the school cafeteria doing homework when suddenly Tia groaned. "I'll *never* be happy," she said.

"What do you mean?" asked Marie. Then she spotted Tia's older sister Jo. She was flirting with some older boys.

"It's so easy for her," Tia moaned. "Meanwhile I'm the only girl in our whole class who's never had a boyfriend."

Marie shrugged. She remembered the shouting match she'd once overheard between Jo and her parents—something about Jo's latest boyfriend. Jo had yelled, "What does God have to do with it anyway? It's my body. I can do what I want."

"Dating is… complicated," said Marie quietly now.

Tia stared at her. "Yeah, but Marie… what if I'm alone for the rest of my life?"

> ★ What would you say to Tia?

* This topic is hard to cover in four pages! You might still have lots of questions by the end. If you want to explore more, try the book *More to the Story* by Jennifer M. Kvamme—it covers a range of questions on attraction, identity, and relationships.

BiBLE TiME:
1 CORiNTHiANS 6 V 12–15, 18–20

12 "I have the right to do anything," you say—but not everything is beneficial. "I have the right to do anything"—but I will not be mastered by anything. 13 You say, "Food for the stomach and the stomach for food, and God will destroy them both." The body, however, is not meant for sexual immorality but for the Lord, and the Lord for the body. 14 By his power God raised the Lord from the dead, and he will raise us also. 15 Do you not know that your bodies are members of Christ himself? Shall I then take the members of Christ and unite them with a prostitute? Never! ...

18 Flee from sexual immorality. All other sins a person commits are outside the body, but whoever sins sexually, sins against their own body. 19 Do you not know that your bodies are temples of the Holy Spirit, who is in you, whom you have received from God? You are not your own; 20 you were bought at a price. Therefore honour God with your bodies.

1. Read 1 Corinthians 6 v 18-20. This is part of a letter written by Paul. What does it mean that our bodies (if we're Christians) are "temples"?

2. How should that affect our attitude towards our own bodies?

3. Read verse 12. "I have the right to do anything" is something people said in Paul's day to justify sleeping around. But what are the two problems Paul highlights with this argument?

4. Read verses 13-15. "Food for the stomach and the stomach for food" is another thing people said to justify sleeping around. Their point was that what you do with your body doesn't matter that much. Why is that incorrect?

5. What good news could you share with Tia from this passage?

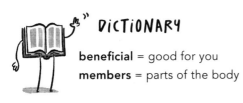 DICTIONARY

beneficial = good for you
members = parts of the body

THINK IT THROUGH

LOVE AND DEVOTION

> ✦ What reasons do people have for wanting a boyfriend or girlfriend, or wanting to get married one day?

Our culture constantly tells us that to be whole or worthwhile we need to have romance or sex. But as Christians we're already whole and worthwhile, loved and secure. We were "bought at a price" and we are "united" with the Lord. We couldn't be closer to Jesus, and nothing is ever going to take his love away.

In fact, part of the point of marriage is to be a picture of that greater relationship that Jesus has with his people (Ephesians 5 v 31-32):

- *When someone makes a sacrifice for their spouse, it's a picture of Jesus' sacrifice for us.*

- *When someone makes a promise to love their spouse as long as they live, it's a picture of the covenant (or agreement) that Jesus has made with us.*

- *When someone experiences the pain of being cheated on, it's a picture of the pain God feels when we are unfaithful to him.*

Why is marriage good? First and foremost it's because it points us to God!

But we can have a complete, full, and fulfilled life regardless of what happens to us romantically—because we have God, who is the person marriage is supposed to point to.

> ✦ What does all of this mean for someone who's dating? What does it mean for someone who's single?

HONOURING GOD

When two people start dating, they become interested in what each other are interested in. They prioritise each other instead of other things. It's the same with our relationship with Jesus. We are his and he is ours. This relationship affects everything else in our lives.

That includes our bodies. Paul says, "The body ... is not meant for sexual immorality but for the Lord". When we do things with our bodies that aren't what God has designed them for, it's as if we're cheating on God.

Our culture tells us to use our bodies for pleasure. Kiss whoever you want, look at porn whenever you want, have sex with whoever you want. "It's fine as long as no one gets hurt." But the Bible says that this isn't true. Physical intimacy is designed to bond married couples together. Outside of marriage, sex is like gluing two pieces of wood together and then tearing them apart. It's not the glue that breaks but the wood. So when God rules out sex outside marriage, he's not trying to stop us having fun but to stop us getting hurt.

> ✦ How would you explain the Christian viewpoint to a friend?

"Sex outside marriage" doesn't just mean sleeping around. Jesus says, "I tell you that anyone who looks at a woman lustfully has already committed adultery with her in his heart" (Matthew 5 v 28). That rules out porn and sexual fantasies.

> ✦ How could you respond if someone invites you to look at porn?

Many people feel ashamed of what they've done with their bodies—or what has been done to them. But we don't need to carry that shame if we are trusting in Jesus. There is no condemnation in him! He loves us deeply and has washed us clean (1 Corinthians 6 v 11).

REFLECT

12. A LIFE THAT SPEAKS

EXPLORING EVANGELISM

MEET RYAN AND JADEN

"Your life is a mess," said Ryan as he and his friend Jaden sat down on the bus. "You'll never sort it all out by yourself."

Jaden grimaced. "All right, all right, it's not like you're any better."

"I am though!" cried Ryan. "Ever since I started going to church and stuff. It's made a massive difference. You can see that, can't you?"

Jaden didn't reply. He just stared out of the bus window.

Ryan took a deep breath. "It's all because of Jesus. He's who you need in your life." He put a hand on Jaden's arm. "I'm serious!"

But Jaden pulled away violently. "Leave me alone. Come on, I don't want to hear it. Don't be so arrogant." He got up and stomped off to take a different seat.

Ryan tried to act like he didn't care, but his cheeks **were** burning **red**. He'd messed it up. *I am NEVER going to try to tell anyone about Jesus ever again,* he thought.

★ What advice would you give to Ryan?

BIBLE TIME:
1 PETER 2 V 9–12 AND 3 V 13–16

2 v 9 But you are a chosen people, a royal priesthood, a holy nation, God's special possession, that you may declare the praises of him who called you out of darkness into his wonderful light. 10 Once you were not a people, but now you are the people of God; once you had not received mercy, but now you have received mercy.

11 Dear friends, I urge you, as foreigners and exiles, to abstain from sinful desires, which wage war against your soul. 12 Live such good lives among the pagans that, though they accuse you of doing wrong, they may see your good deeds and glorify God on the day he visits us. …

3 v 13 Who is going to harm you if you are eager to do good? 14 But even if you should suffer for what is right, you are blessed. "Do not fear their threats; do not be frightened." 15 But in your hearts revere Christ as Lord. Always be prepared to give an answer to everyone who asks you to give the reason for the hope that you have. But do this with gentleness and respect, 16 keeping a clear conscience, so that those who speak maliciously against your good behaviour in Christ may be ashamed of their slander.

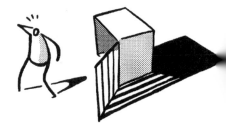

1. Read 1 Peter 2 v 9-12. What does Peter say about our identity as Christians? (You could underline the key phrases.)

2. What does this mean for how we should live?

3. Read 3 v 13-16 and look again at 2 v 12. What responses can we expect when we speak about Jesus?

4. What should our attitude be when we speak about Jesus?

5. Do you think Ryan was doing what Peter said?

 DICTIONARY

priesthood = special people set apart in order to represent God
foreigners and exiles = people who don't really belong in this world
abstain from = keep away from
pagans = people who don't believe in Jesus
glorify = praise
revere = be very respectful towards
maliciously = with the intention of harming someone
slander = lies

THINK IT THROUGH

BEAUTIFUL PEOPLE

Christians are attractive people. Knowing Jesus makes us less selfish and more loving. We're not perfect of course, but when there is real change in us, people notice the difference. We're becoming attractive people—people who attract others to Jesus.

We persuade people of the truth about Jesus partly by living good lives and doing good deeds. Peter tells us to be ready "to give the reason for the hope that [we] have"—i.e. to talk about our faith. But the thing that's going to prompt people to ask questions about our faith is a life that displays our hope in Jesus.

✦ Think of some Christians you know who live like this. What is it about them that you admire?

✦ If you're a Christian, how do you think knowing Jesus impacts the way you live?

Thankfully the pressure is not all on you. Just before we're told to be ready to give a reason for our hope, we're told, "*All of you*, be like-minded, be sympathetic, love one another, be compassionate and humble" (3 v 8). The love and unity of Christians together, as a church family, is important—it's a powerful sign of hope. It's often the shared life of a church that gets people asking questions. The chances are that there's nowhere else in your neighbourhood where such a diverse group of people come together to be family. So look for opportunities to introduce people to your church family.

BEAUTIFUL WORDS

Attractive lives are important, but they're not enough. People need the good news of Jesus, and by definition "news" is something to declare with words.

You may not be able to preach a sermon, but you can tell people what Jesus has done for you. Or you can invite them to come to church, or to read one of the Gospels where they can meet Jesus for themselves.

* Think of a non-Christian friend and imagine what you might say to them about what Jesus has done for you. Can you sum it up in three sentences?

Notice that we're supposed to tell people about Jesus "with gentleness and respect" (3 v 15). It's tempting to feel defensive and so end up getting angry. But it's not our job to win the argument. Our job is simply to speak of Jesus as clearly as we can. The rest we can leave to the Holy Spirit.

The good news of Jesus is good news—not bad news. Jesus has defeated sin and death to give us forgiveness and eternal life. And he offers hope for this life and the life to come. That's news worth sharing!

* Why might people sometimes not want to hear this good news?

The true reason for people not wanting to hear about Jesus is that they want to rule over their own lives instead of letting God do it. We all naturally think like that because of sin. Thankfully, the Holy Spirit opens people's eyes to see the glory and grace of Jesus. It can be our privilege as Christians to see that supernatural work take place right in front of us!

REFLECT

ACTIVITIES AND REFLECTIONS

1. JESUS WINS: EXPLORING THE GOSPEL

Activity: Play a game or hold a competition. There's a bag of sweets for the winner—but when they win, they'll share the prize with everyone.

Reflection: Pick a song that worships Jesus for his death and resurrection, and listen to it together. Two reflection questions for the group to think about while they listen (or write answers on the **Reflect** page):

- Do you ever find yourself thinking, "I'm just bad" or "I can never make up for that bad thing I did", or being haunted by guilty or shameful memories? Imagine all of that being washed away by the work of Jesus.

- Who do you know who may have misunderstood what being a Christian is? Is there any way you could help them think about it in a different way?

2. EMPTY HANDS: EXPLORING GRACE

Activity: Set the group one or more of the following tasks:

- Put a rubber glove or balloon over your nose, with the opening pressed against your skin. (Make sure the mouth is left free.) Then try to blow it up using just air from your nose.

- Put a blindfold on, balance ten books on your head, and make it from one side of the room to the other without dropping any.

- Eat 6 dry crackers (cream crackers or saltine crackers) in one minute.

- Spin in a circle 10 times then walk in a perfectly straight line.

The point is, they're too hard... just like it's too hard for humans to please God on their own.

Give everyone a prize anyway!

Reflection: Ask everyone to draw round both their hands on a piece of paper (or on the **Reflect** page if they have small hands). Underneath one they should write GRACE, and underneath the other, GOOD WORKS. Explain the following:

The GRACE one represents the empty hands we bring to Jesus. You could write a prayer in it—maybe saying sorry for some things you regret, and/or thanking him for his grace to you.

The GOOD WORKS hand represents the good works God has prepared for us to do. Take a moment to quietly pray and ask God to show you what good works he has prepared for you to do this week. You could write down your prayer or some of the good works you think you could do.

3. PART OF THE FAMILY: EXPLORING CHURCH

Activity: Here's a challenge to illustrate teamwork. Everyone has to stand on a rug or mat. Now you have to turn the rug over (i.e. upside down)—but without anyone's feet touching the ground.

Reflection: Spend time in groups praying for each other. Give everyone a moment to think of what they'd like prayer for this week. Could be a "Christian thing" or not. Share them all and then go round and pray for each other.

4. CHILDREN, NOT SLAVES: EXPLORING OBEDIENCE

Activity: Play two games of Simon Says. In the first game, the leader is very kind and it's easy to obey. In the second game, the leader is making it very difficult to obey. This is a simple way of illustrating how, when we know that God loves us, it's easier to obey him.

Reflection: Ask the group to think through the following questions quietly, on their own or in pairs.

• What temptations do you struggle with?

• Do you ever find yourself resenting God or his law?

• What truths could you turn to in these situations?

Using the **Reflect** page, they may like to write a thank-you prayer to Jesus for dying on the cross so that we can be adopted as God's children.

5. ROOT AND BRANCH: EXPLORING OUR UNION WITH CHRIST

Activity: Stand up and form a circle (you need to stand fairly close together). Everyone stretch your hands into the middle. Then every hand needs to grab another hand (make sure you're grabbing the hands of two different people!). Now you're all connected to each other, you need to try to unwind the tangle. Without letting go of anyone's hands, see if you can get so that you're all standing in a circle again.

Reflection: As a group, share practical ideas about how to connect with Jesus. Then make a plan together—what is one thing you can all do this week that will help you connect with Jesus in a way that energises your faith? Or you may even be able to put something into practice right now.

6. HOPE AND GLORY: EXPLORING SUFFERING

Activity: Set some challenges that involve waiting and endurance. First, tell everyone to stand with their eyes closed. They have to count 30 seconds. When they think 30 seconds is over, they sit down. Whoever is closest to the real 30 seconds wins a prize. This feels longer than you'd think! Second, do the same thing but this time everyone needs to hold a plank position for the 30 seconds.

You could also do some more straightforward endurance competitions—who can hold a plank for the longest, who can hold both arms out for the longest, and so on.

Reflection: Learn Romans 8 v 38-39 together. You could create a doodle of it and colour it in, or make up a song version. (You can also find a printable colouring page of this verse by going to www.thegoodbook.co.uk/life-with-jesus-youth-edition.)

Leave time as well to pray for some people you know who are suffering.

7. GOD SPEAKS: EXPLORING THE BIBLE

Activity: Play Murder in the Dark. Everyone needs to shut their eyes while a leader chooses a murderer, then a police officer, by tapping two people on the shoulder. Nobody must know who they are! Clear the room and switch off the lights. Everyone has to walk around the room carefully. The murderer has to tap other players on the shoulder, silently killing them. If you've been killed, fall to the ground—make dramatic noises if you like! If you stumble into someone who's been killed, shout "Murder in the dark!" Everyone must freeze. Then switch the lights back on and survey the damage. The police officer has two guesses to find the murderer. If the police officer has been killed or the murderer isn't identified, the murderer wins.

Bonus points to anyone who can spot the link with the passage—which is the light and darkness metaphor that Peter uses in verse 19.

Reflection: Discuss one or both of the following questions:

- Do you have a favourite Bible verse? Share it with the group.

- Is there anything that holds you back from reading the Bible? Could you think how to get help with that?

Finish by spending some time worshipping God for the gift of his word. You could listen to a song or just say some prayers.

8. A FATHER WHO LISTENS: EXPLORING PRAYER

Activity: Give everyone a name which they must keep secret. All the names are in father-child pairs (either in real life or from a film). Then everyone wanders around the room trying to find their father or child by asking each other yes/no questions. For example, if you're Simba, you might ask someone if they're from a Disney film. They can sit down once they've found their partner.

As an extension, ask what makes these fathers different to each other, and what makes God different to them all. Clarifying what kind of father God is (and is not) will be particularly helpful for those who have a difficult or non-existent relationship with their earthly father.

Reflection: Make a colourful "prayer wall" together using a large sheet of paper or board and some coloured pens. Assign one colour to each of the seven parts of the Lord's Prayer. Everyone must write prayers that link to each theme using the correct colours.

9. GIVE ME A SIGN: EXPLORING COMMUNION

Activity: Play a memory game. Stand in a circle—make sure you've got space to move. The first person does an action or makes a sign with their hands that everyone can copy. The second person has to repeat that action and add their own. The third person repeats the first two actions and adds a third. See how far you can get around the circle before people start forgetting the actions.

Reflection: Invite everyone to make their own sign of Jesus' promises and presence. They could simply draw something that looks a bit like a road sign, on the **Reflect** page or separately. Or devise some actions, a bit like sign language. (Or look up some actual sign language and learn how to sign some key words that have to do with Communion.)

Then spend some time saying some short thank-you prayers.

10. TREASURE HUNT: EXPLORING MONEY

Activity: Divide into two teams. One team needs to leave the room while the other team hides some "treasure". The first team can then come in and try to find it. Next, swap over. Which team can come up with the best hiding place, and which team is the best at finding it?

Reflection: Get everybody to find a space of their own for some quiet reflection on the following questions.

• What is your attitude to money? Does anything need to change?

• What do you want to thank Jesus for?

• What specific act of generosity could you do this week?

It could be helpful to write down a prayer. Or create a doodle based on 2 Corinthians 8 v 9. (You can find a printable colouring page of this verse by going to www.thegoodbook.co.uk/life-with-jesus-youth-edition.)

11. TRUE LOVE: EXPLORING ROMANCE

Activity: Make small models of greater realities, using modelling clay or similar. The young people might make a model of a famous monument or something else tangible, or they could try more abstract sculptures that represent concepts like love or friendship. (Depending on the group, you may want to come up with your own list of things to sculpt in advance!) Gather a list of the concepts or things that the models represent, line up all the finished models, read out the list, and see if the young people can guess which model corresponds to which greater reality.

Finish with a reminder that marriage is designed as a model of the greater reality of Christians' relationship with Jesus.

Reflection: Give the group paper so that they can all make a people paper chain. You only need two people in each chain. One is you and one is Jesus. Spend some time decorating your people however you want, but leave space for a short prayer based on something you've talked about today.

12. A LiFE THAT SPEAKS: EXPLORiNG EVANGELiSM

Activity: Play the game Telephone (or Operator, or Chinese Whispers). Each whisper needs to be something that the whisperer considers to be good news. (But it can be made-up.)

Reflection: 1 Peter 2 v 9 tells us, "Declare the praises of him who called you out of darkness into his wonderful light."

Put that into practice now. Switch the lights out and put some quiet worship music on in the background. Then it's a prayer free-for-all: shout out prayers of praise to Jesus, short or long, anything you like. Invite the group to think about what it means that he called us out of darkness into the light.

Finally, ask everyone to think of a friend or family member who they wish knew about Jesus. As the lights go on again, pray for those people quietly and ask God to provide opportunities to share the good news with them.

You can also find a printable colouring page of 1 Peter 2 v 9 by going to www.thegoodbook.co.uk/life-with-jesus-youth-edition.

the good book
COMPANY

BIBLICAL | RELEVANT | ACCESSIBLE

At The Good Book Company we are dedicated to helping Christians and local churches grow. We believe that God's growth process always starts with hearing clearly what he has said to us through his timeless and flawless word—the Bible.

Ever since we opened our doors in 1991, we have been striving to produce resources that are biblical, relevant, and accessible. By God's grace, we have grown to become an international publisher, encouraging ordinary Christians of every age and stage and every background and denomination to live for Christ day by day and equipping churches to grow in their knowledge of God, their love for one another, and the effectiveness of their outreach.

Call one of our friendly team for a discussion of your needs or visit one of our local websites for more information on the resources and services we provide.

Your friends at The Good Book Company

thegoodbook.com | thegoodbook.co.uk
thegoodbook.com.au | thegoodbook.co.nz
thegoodbook.co.in